Super
SUBMARINES

To Edward Stansfield (aka Ed) with bubbles—T. M.
For My—A. P.

KINGFISHER
LONDON & NEW YORK

Text copyright © Tony Mitton 2006
Illustrations copyright © Ant Parker 2006

Published in the United States by Kingfisher, 175 Fifth Ave., New York, NY 10010
Kingfisher is an imprint of Macmillan Children's Books, London.

Distributed in the U.S. and Canada by Macmillan,
175 Fifth Ave., New York, NY 10010

Library of Congress Cataloging-in-Publication data has been applied for.

ISBN: 978-0-7534-7208-8

Kingfisher books are available for special promotions and premiums.
For details contact: Special Markets Department,
Macmillan, 175 Fifth Avenue, New York, NY 10010.
For more information, please visit www.kingfisherpublications.com

Printed in China
10 9 8 7 6 5 4 3 2 1
1TR/0614/LFG/-/128MA

Super
SUBMARINES

Tony Mitton
and
Ant Parker

KINGFISHER
NEW YORK

A submarine's a type of boat that dives beneath the sea.

Below the waves is such a strange
and wondrous place to be.

To dive, it takes in water until its tanks are full.

The weight of water gives the submarine a downward pull.

When it's underwater,
the propeller makes it go.
The hydroplanes can tilt to steer it
up or down, like so.

The rudder also steers the sub
and turns it left or right.
Computers help navigate—
down deep, there's not much light.

The periscope can poke above
the waves to peer around,

but farther down, the submarine
depends on sonar sound.

The sonar sends a signal out—
a special type of beep

that bounces back to help them guess
what's out there in the deep.

A submarine must have a crew
to run it night and day.

The crew needs living quarters,
where they eat and rest and play.

Submersibles are different subs
that probe the deepest ocean.
Down that far, it's still and dark.
There's hardly any motion.

But, even there, submersibles
discover deep-sea creatures
that glow or carry lanterns
and have very funny features.

Submersibles are used to rescue
divers or explore.
They sometimes salvage sunken wrecks
upon the ocean floor.

They're used to service oil rigs,
lay cables, and fix pipes.
Their robot subs have cameras
and arms of many types.

But look! Our sub is rising—
its work below is done.

Very soon the busy crew
will see the sky and sun.

Its ballast tanks have emptied—
they've pushed the water out.

The submarine is back in dock.
"Hooray!" the sailors shout.

Submarine parts

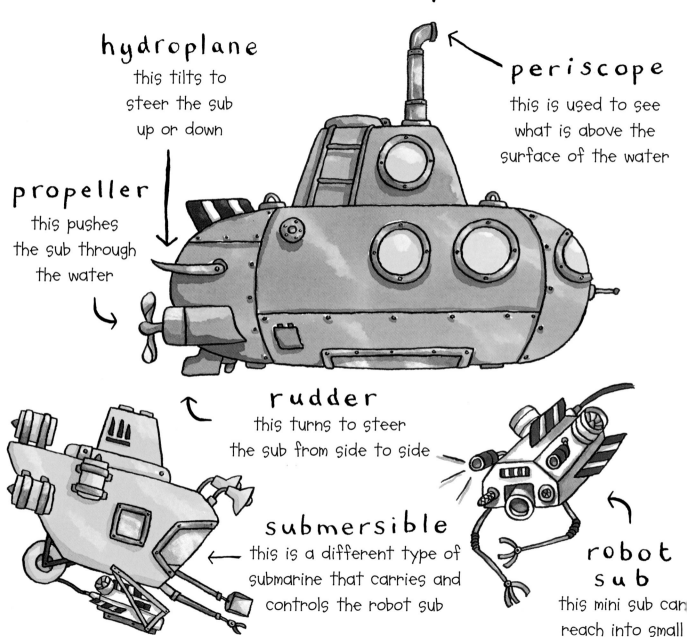

hydroplane
this tilts to steer the sub up or down

periscope
this is used to see what is above the surface of the water

propeller
this pushes the sub through the water

rudder
this turns to steer the sub from side to side

submersible
this is a different type of submarine that carries and controls the robot sub

robot sub
this mini sub can reach into small and narrow space